# The Heart
## in Action

**Richard Walker**

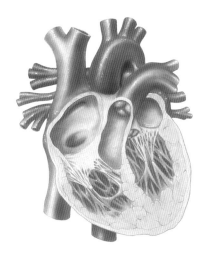

**W**

**FRANKLIN WATTS**

LONDON•SYDNEY

First published in 2004 by Franklin Watts
96 Leonard Street, London EC2A 4XD

Franklin Watts Australia
45–51 Huntley Street
Alexandria, NSW 2015

Series editor: Adrian Cole
Editor: Andrew Campbell
Series design: White Design
Art director: Jonathan Hair
Picture researcher: Diana Morris
Educational consultants: Peter Riley and Beverley Goodger
Medical consultant: Dr Gabrielle Murphy

A CIP catalogue record for this book
is available from the British Library.

ISBN: 0 7496 5135 0

Printed in Malaysia

Acknowledgements:
Special thanks to our model Imani Jawarah
Alex Bartel/SPL: 19b. CNRI/SPL: 22t, 24b. Custom Medical Stockphoto/
SPL: 9b.Eye of Science/SPL: 6c, 11t, 21b. Pascal Goetgheluck/SPL: 25b. P. Hattenburger/
Publiphoto Diffusion/SPL: 6b. Laboratory of Molecular Biology,
MRC/SPL: 20b. Dr. P. Marazzi/SPL: 27b. Prof. P. Motta/Department of Anatomy,
University "La Sapienza", Rome/SPL:22b, 23b. Chris Priest/SPL: 19t.
Saturn Stills/SPL: 29b. David Scharf/SPL: 24t. SPL: 9c, 13b, 16t, 17b,
21t, 22c, 23t. Alexander Tsiara/SPL: 17t.

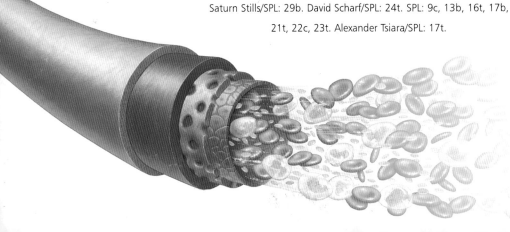

# Contents

# The heart is a living pump
## that never gets tired

**O**nce people thought the heart made us fall in love. In fact, the heart is a living pump that pushes a red liquid called blood around the body. An adult human heart does this about 70 times a minute, without stopping for rest. In an average lifetime, a person's heart beats approximately 3 billion times.

### Where is the heart?

The heart lies in the middle of the chest, a few centimetres under the skin, protected by the ribcage. It sits between the left and right lungs with its tip pointing down, towards the left side of the body. Your heart is about the size of your clenched fist.

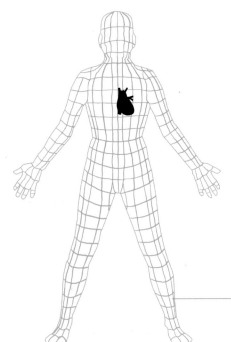

**The position of the heart**

*The heart, as well as the lungs, lies protected inside the bony ribcage.*

## NEVER TIRING

Ask a group of friends to open their hand, then clench their fist. Using a watch with a second hand to record the time, get them to repeat this every second until they cannot carry on. The muscles that clench and unclench the fist soon get tired. This is because they are skeletal muscles. In contrast, the cardiac muscle in your heart – which also contracts about once every second – never tires.

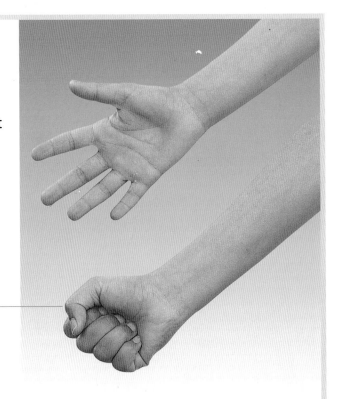

**Open and close**

*Clench and unclench your fist with plenty of force once every second.*

## Parts of the heart

The heart is actually two pumps, one on the left side and one on the right. Each side is divided into two 'chambers': a smaller, thin-walled atrium on top and a larger, thick-walled ventricle below. Each atrium receives blood entering the heart, while each ventricle pumps blood out of the heart.

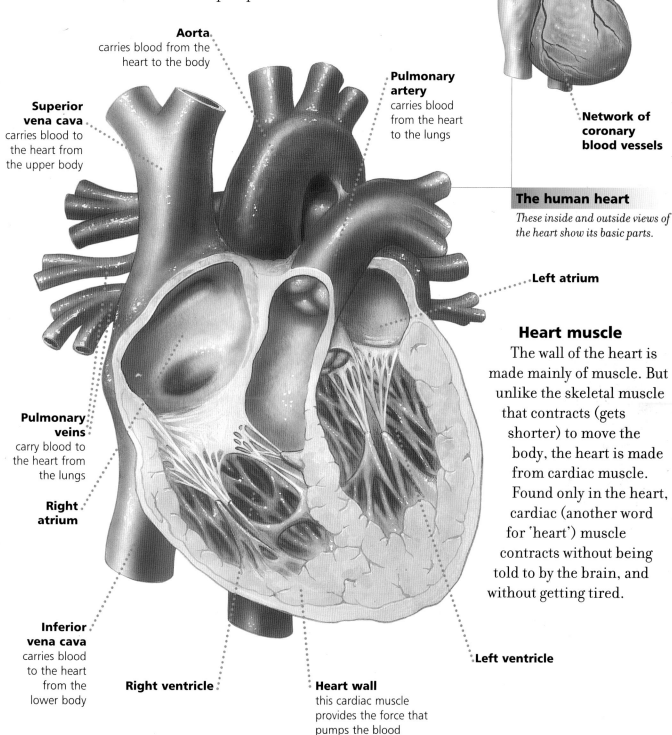

**Aorta**
carries blood from the heart to the body

**Superior vena cava**
carries blood to the heart from the upper body

**Pulmonary artery**
carries blood from the heart to the lungs

**Network of coronary blood vessels**

**The human heart**
*These inside and outside views of the heart show its basic parts.*

**Left atrium**

**Pulmonary veins**
carry blood to the heart from the lungs

**Right atrium**

**Inferior vena cava**
carries blood to the heart from the lower body

**Right ventricle**

**Heart wall**
this cardiac muscle provides the force that pumps the blood

**Left ventricle**

## Heart muscle

The wall of the heart is made mainly of muscle. But unlike the skeletal muscle that contracts (gets shorter) to move the body, the heart is made from cardiac muscle. Found only in the heart, cardiac (another word for 'heart') muscle contracts without being told to by the brain, and without getting tired.

# The heart makes blood move
## around the body

The heart moves blood through the body, every second of every day. Whether we are running around, sitting in a chair or even fast asleep, the heart pumps blood all around the body. Together, the heart and blood help keep the body alive and active.

### Circulatory system

The human body is made of trillions of tiny living units called cells. Blood flows past these cells and keeps them working properly. To reach those cells, blood is pumped by the heart along tubes called blood vessels. The heart, blood vessels and blood make up the circulatory system, so-called because blood circulates (goes round) the body.

**Blood cells**
*Blood contains cells of its own, as this microscopic view of red blood cells shows.*

**A living pump**
*The heart beats non-stop to keep life giving blood circulating round the body to the cells (see page 8).*

6

## River of life

Blood keeps the body working properly in three ways. Firstly, it delivers glucose, oxygen and other essentials to the cells, and removes their wastes. Secondly, it keeps the cells warm. And thirdly, it helps protect the body against bacteria and other disease-causing germs.

## How much blood?

On average, the body contains 5 litres of blood – that's around 8 per cent of the total body weight. The body makes new blood all the time, to replace old blood cells that can no longer perform effectively. When someone loses a small amount of blood, for example from a small cut, the body soon makes up the loss. If they lose a lot of blood, they will need to get help at a hospital (see page 19).

### A lot of bottle

*The average person contains the same amount of blood as five 1-litre bottles.*

## YOUR HEART AT WORK

You will need a watch or clock with a second hand. Sit quietly, then find your pulse, as shown. This is produced by your heart pumping blood along a blood vessel called an artery. Count the number of beats in 15 seconds. Multiply it by 4 to give the number of heartbeats per minute. Get your friends to measure their heartbeats as well, and compare the results on a bar chart.

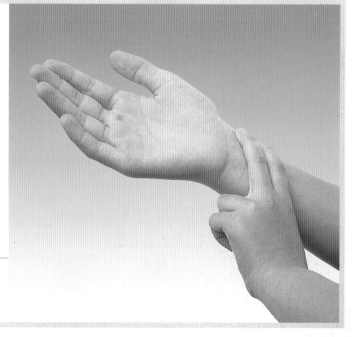

### Finding your pulse

*Press the tips of two fingers lightly on the inside of your wrist, just below your thumb.*

# Blood travels through a system
# **of blood vessels**

**B**lood flows round and round the body along blood vessels. The network of blood vessels reaches all parts of the body, including the bones, brain, mouth and muscles. If blood vessels in an adult's body could be laid end to end, they would extend for an incredible 150,000 kilometres.

## Two circulations

There are actually two circulation routes in the body, linked by the heart. One route carries blood poor in oxygen from the heart to the lungs to pick up oxygen, and takes the oxygen-rich blood back to the heart. The other route delivers blood rich in oxygen from the heart to the head, liver and other parts of the body, and then returns oxygen-poor blood to the heart, ready for the next trip to the lungs.

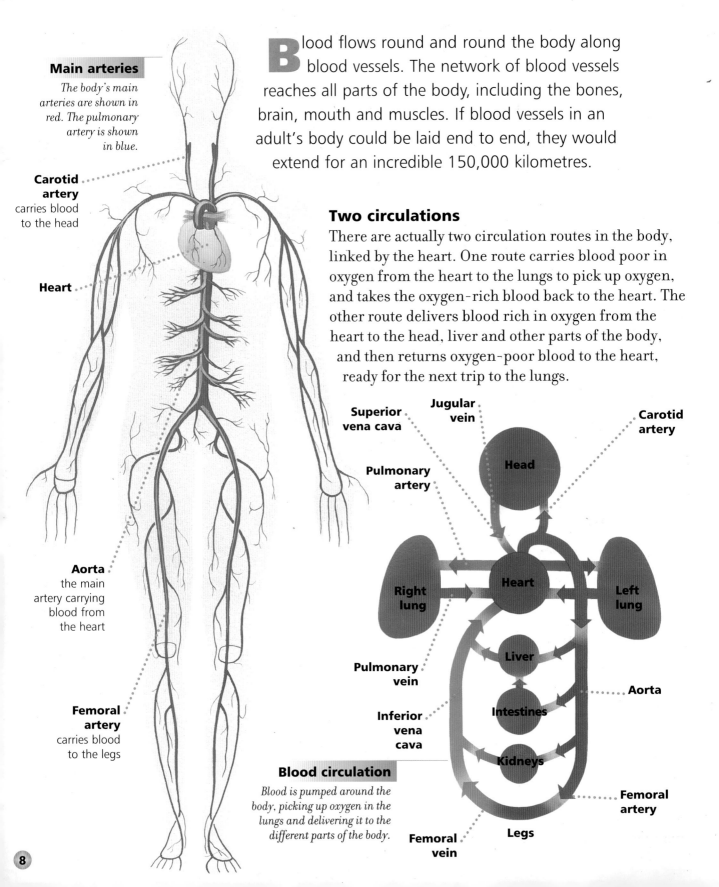

**Main arteries**

*The body's main arteries are shown in red. The pulmonary artery is shown in blue.*

**Carotid artery**
carries blood to the head

**Heart**

**Aorta**
the main artery carrying blood from the heart

**Femoral artery**
carries blood to the legs

**Superior vena cava**

**Jugular vein**

**Carotid artery**

**Pulmonary artery**

**Head**

**Right lung**

**Heart**

**Left lung**

**Pulmonary vein**

**Liver**

**Inferior vena cava**

**Intestines**

**Aorta**

**Kidneys**

**Femoral artery**

**Blood circulation**

*Blood is pumped around the body, picking up oxygen in the lungs and delivering it to the different parts of the body.*

**Femoral vein**

**Legs**

## HARVEY'S DISCOVERY

Until the 17th century, many people believed that blood moved backwards and forwards along blood vessels, like the tide going in and out. An English doctor called William Harvey (1578–1657) did lots of experiments that proved that blood circulates in a continuous direction around the body, pumped by the heart. He showed that valves inside veins stopped blood from flowing backwards, in a similar way to closing doors.

### Dr William Harvey

*This engraving shows Dr William Harvey (centre left) during a lecture on blood circulation. Harvey showed that blood flows in one direction only.*

### Angiogram

*This angiogram shows the left carotid artery (the thick red vessel at the bottom), one of the major arteries that supplies blood to the head.*

## Seeing blood vessels

Doctors can view a person's blood vessels using a special type of X-ray. A dye (seen on the right in red) is injected into the blood vessel to make it stand out in the X-ray. Then an X-ray photograph called an angiogram (meaning a 'vessel picture') is taken. Angiograms allow doctors to spot anything that may be wrong with a blood vessel.

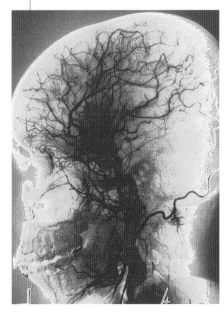

### Main veins

*The body's main veins are shown in blue. The pulmonary veins are shown in red.*

**Jugular vein**
carries blood from the head

**Pulmonary veins**
carry blood from the lungs to the heart

**Inferior vena cava**
carries blood from the lower body

**Femoral vein**
carries blood from the legs

# Three types of blood vessel perform **different tasks**

**B**lood vessels are the body's transport system. The 'major roads' are the big arteries and veins. The 'minor roads' are the smaller arteries and veins that fan out to different parts of the body. The 'backstreets' are the capillaries, which supply blood to every cell in the body and connect arteries and veins.

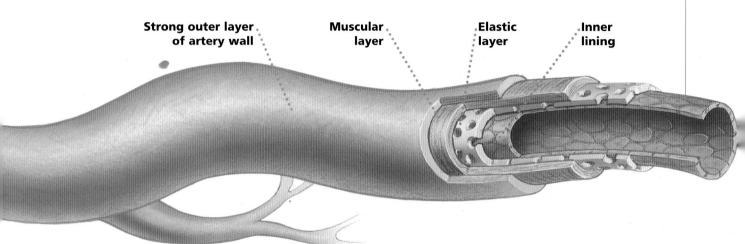

**Strong outer layer of artery wall** · **Muscular layer** · **Elastic layer** · **Inner lining**

## Arteries

Arteries carry blood away from the heart. The walls of arteries are thick, so they do not burst when blood is pumped along them under high pressure by the heart. They are also stretchy, so they can bulge as blood surges through them and then 'spring' back.

## Veins

Veins carry blood towards the heart. Veins have much thinner walls than arteries because the blood returning to the heart is at a lower pressure. Because this blood has less 'push', many veins have valves that stop blood flowing backwards, away from the heart.

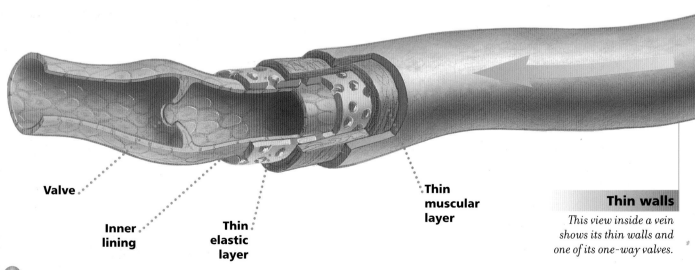

**Valve** · **Inner lining** · **Thin elastic layer** · **Thin muscular layer**

## Capillaries

As arteries fan out from the heart, they divide to form smaller and smaller 'backstreets'. The smallest, called arterioles, split into capillaries that are just $0.01$ mm across. Capillaries form a massive network that carries blood past all body cells, supplying them with oxygen and glucose and removing waste carbon dioxide. Having done their job, capillaries join up to form tiny veins called venules. These unite to form bigger and bigger veins that run back to the heart.

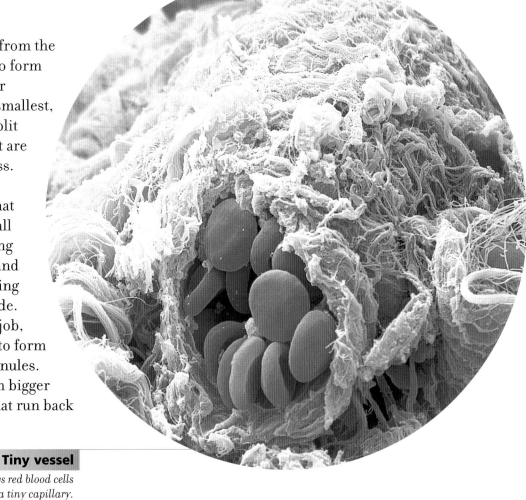

**Tiny vessel**

*This micrograph shows red blood cells passing through a tiny capillary.*

### VEIN VALVES

Ask an adult to put their hand flat on a table. Look for the veins standing out on the back of their hand. Put one of your fingers on one end of a vein near to their knuckles. Then use a second finger to stroke the vein towards their elbow. This pushes blood past a valve, back towards the heart, and empties the vein. Lift your second finger. The vein should remain flat and empty because a valve stops blood flowing backwards and your finger stops blood flowing in. This is similar to an experiment carried out by Dr William Harvey (see page 9).

## Aorta and vena cava

The biggest of the arteries is the aorta, the main route for oxygen-rich blood leaving the heart. The biggest vein is the vena cava, which carries oxygen-poor blood back to the heart. Both the aorta and the vena cava are $2.5$ cm across – about $2,500$ times wider than the smallest capillary.

Aorta

**Thick and thin**

Vena cava

*Although both the aorta and vena cava are about $2.5$ cm wide, the venae cavae have thinner walls.*

# The heartbeat cycle pushes blood **through the heart**

**E**very time the heart beats it pumps blood along the blood vessels. The heart is so powerful that it pumps the blood inside the body all the way around about once every minute. Blood flows into and out of the heart as part of a cycle, producing the sounds we hear when we listen to someone's heart.

## Flowing through the heart

When blood has circulated through the body it returns to the heart. This oxygen-poor blood enters the right atrium. It then passes into the right ventricle before being pumped out along the pulmonary arteries to the lungs. Oxygen-rich blood from the lungs enters the left atrium through pulmonary veins.

Oxygen-rich blood then passes into the left ventricle before being pumped out through the aorta to the rest of the body. Valves between each atrium and ventricle, and guarding the exit from each ventricle, make sure that blood only flows in one direction.

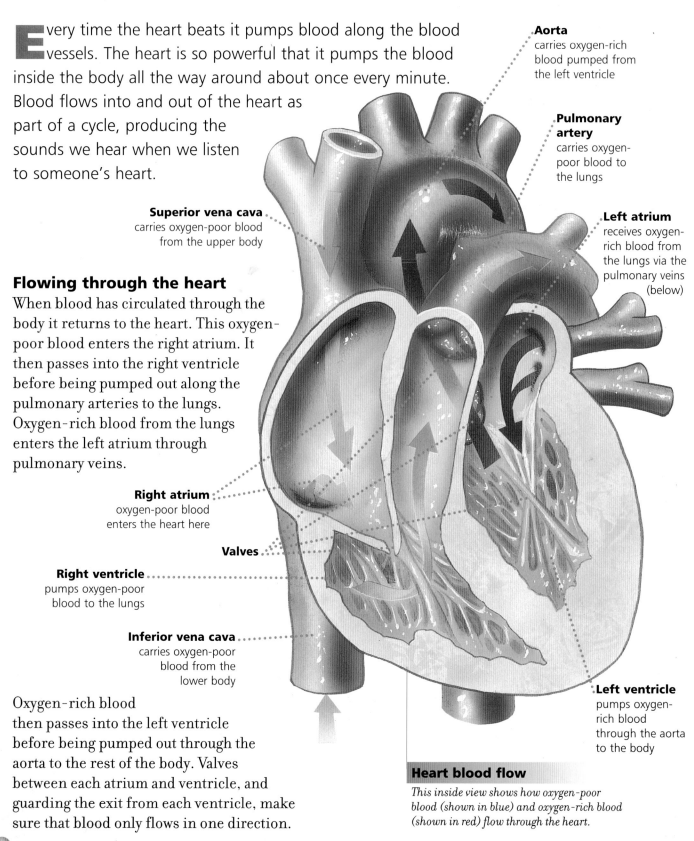

**Aorta**
carries oxygen-rich blood pumped from the left ventricle

**Pulmonary artery**
carries oxygen-poor blood to the lungs

**Left atrium**
receives oxygen-rich blood from the lungs via the pulmonary veins (below)

**Superior vena cava**
carries oxygen-poor blood from the upper body

**Right atrium**
oxygen-poor blood enters the heart here

**Valves**

**Right ventricle**
pumps oxygen-poor blood to the lungs

**Inferior vena cava**
carries oxygen-poor blood from the lower body

**Left ventricle**
pumps oxygen-rich blood through the aorta to the body

**Heart blood flow**

*This inside view shows how oxygen-poor blood (shown in blue) and oxygen-rich blood (shown in red) flow through the heart.*

## Heartbeat cycle

A heartbeat is made up of three stages. Together they form the heartbeat cycle, which repeats itself about once every second. In the first stage (1), the heart relaxes and blood fills the two atria (the plural of atrium). The valves at the openings into the pulmonary artery and aorta close to stop blood flowing backwards. Next (2), the atria contract and push blood into the ventricles. Finally (3), the ventricles contract, pushing blood out of the heart. The valves between the ventricles and the atria close to stop blood going back into the atria.

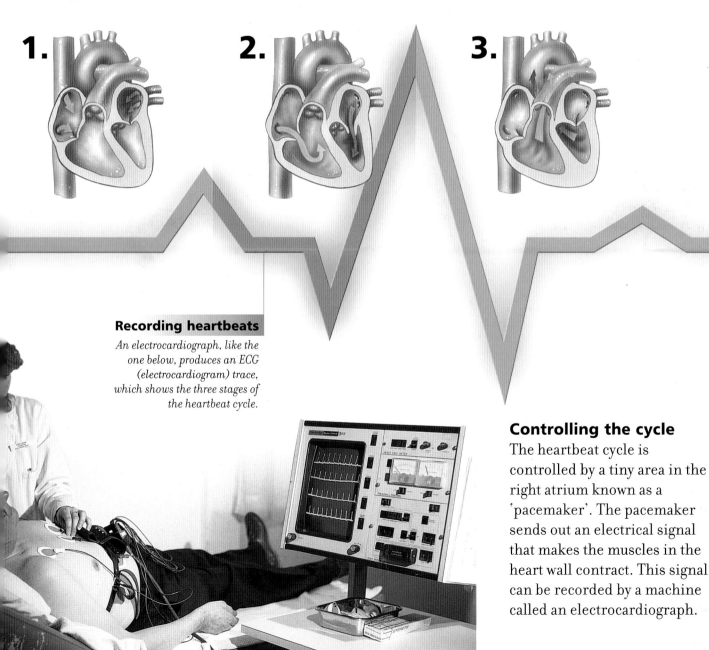

**1.**  **2.**  **3.**

### Recording heartbeats

*An electrocardiograph, like the one below, produces an ECG (electrocardiogram) trace, which shows the three stages of the heartbeat cycle.*

## Controlling the cycle

The heartbeat cycle is controlled by a tiny area in the right atrium known as a 'pacemaker'. The pacemaker sends out an electrical signal that makes the muscles in the heart wall contract. This signal can be recorded by a machine called an electrocardiograph.

# The heart beats faster
## during exercise

Compare jumping in the air with watching TV. Which activity uses muscles more? The answer, of course, is the first activity. Whenever we exercise, the muscles work harder, and to do that they need extra energy. To supply this energy, the heart beats faster to supply more blood to the muscles.

**Faster heart beat**

*As this athlete runs, her heart beats faster to keep up with the demands of her hard-working muscles.*

**Recording a heart rate**

*This graph shows how heart rate increases during exercise, and then slowly returns to normal after exercise.*

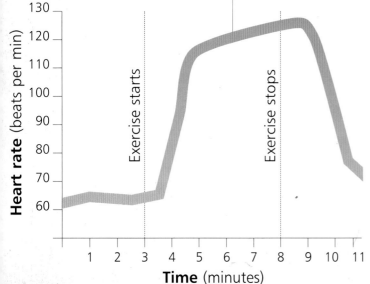

**Heart rate (beats per min)**

130
120
110
100
90
80
70
60

Exercise starts

Exercise stops

1  2  3  4  5  6  7  8  9  10  11

**Time** (minutes)

## On the move

Muscles, like other body tissues, get their energy from glucose. Inside a muscle cell, glucose is broken down with the help of oxygen. This process is called cell respiration. It releases energy from glucose, but also produces waste carbon dioxide. The energy is used to make muscles contract. When we start to exercise, the heart automatically speeds up to get more blood containing oxygen and glucose to the muscles, and to remove more carbon dioxide. To help this, the blood arteries supplying the muscles get wider. After exercise, the heart automatically begins to slow down.

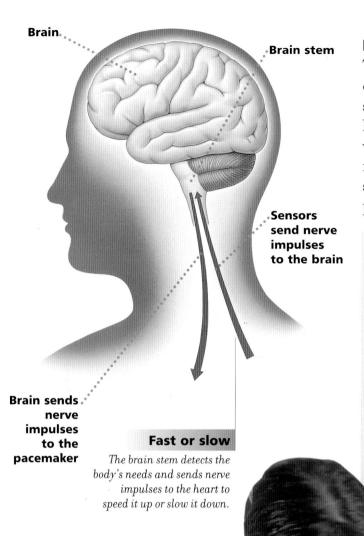

**Brain**

**Brain stem**

**Sensors send nerve impulses to the brain**

**Brain sends nerve impulses to the pacemaker**

### Fast or slow

*The brain stem detects the body's needs and sends nerve impulses to the heart to speed it up or slow it down.*

## In control

The heart beats faster during exercise because of sensors in certain blood vessels. These sensors detect the extra carbon dioxide in the blood that has been produced by the hard-working muscles. The sensors then send nerve impulses to the brain. The brain automatically sends messages to the heart's pacemaker (see page 13), telling it to make the heart beat faster.

### RUNNING PULSE

You will need a watch or a clock with a second hand. You have already seen how to measure your pulse rate (see page 7). Now see how it changes during exercise. First measure your pulse at rest. Then run on the spot for 2 minutes. Immediately measure your pulse rate again. Rest, and measure your pulse rate after another 2 minutes. Plot your results on a bar chart, and compare them with those of your friends.

## Under pressure

Every time the heart's ventricles contract, they cause blood to surge through the arteries and push against the artery walls. This pushing is known as blood pressure. During exercise, the heart beats faster and more forcefully, so blood pressure goes up. Blood pressure can be measured using a sphygmomanometer (a 'pulse pressure measurer').

### Measuring pressure

*This person is having their blood pressure measured by a doctor.*

# The heart has its own
# blood supply system

Like any other part of the body, the heart needs a constant supply of oxygen and glucose to keep it alive and make it work. But blood pumped by the heart rushes through it too fast for the heart muscle to pick up its vital supplies. Instead, the heart relies on its very own blood supply.

### Coronary arteries

The heart's blood supply is called the coronary circulation. Left and right coronary arteries branch off from the aorta and fan out over and through the cardiac muscle in the heart's wall. The blood they carry provides the oxygen and glucose demanded by the hard-working muscle cells. After it has done its job, the oxygen-poor blood is collected by a large vein that empties into the right atrium.

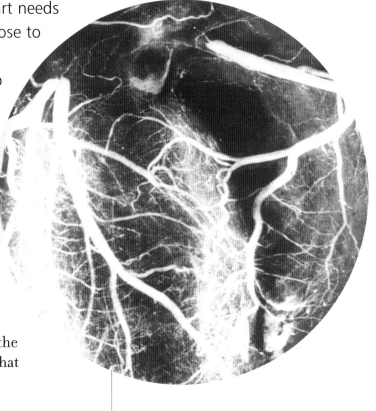

### Heart's own supply

*This angiogram shows the heart's coronary arteries.*

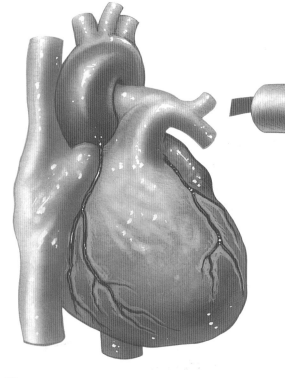

### Slowing the flow

*A fatty build-up in this coronary blood vessel slows the blood flow to the heart.*

### Narrowed vessels

As people get older, their coronary arteries can get narrower. This is because fatty substances may build up inside them. If a narrowed coronary artery becomes blocked, it cuts off the blood supply to one part of the heart's muscle. This damages the muscle and can cause a heart attack, which may kill the person.

## A NEW HEART

Today, badly damaged hearts can sometimes be replaced by a heart transplant. This involves taking a healthy heart from someone who has died (often as a result of an accident) and using it to replace a damaged heart. The person who receives the heart takes special drugs to stop their immune system (see pages 28–29) rejecting their new heart because it is not originally from their body.

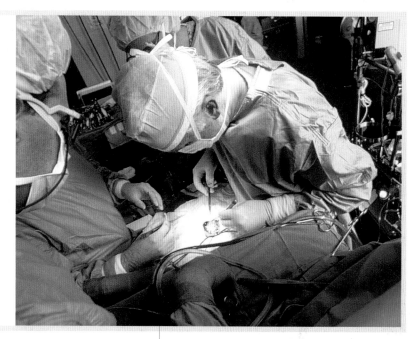

**Narrowed artery**

**Open heart surgery**

*These surgeons are performing an operation to replace a patient's heart. They use a mechanical heart to circulate the blood while the patient is unconscious.*

**Danger signs**

*This angiogram shows a narrowed coronary artery caused by a build-up in fatty deposits.*

## Healthy heart

The chances of having blocked coronary arteries can be greatly reduced by following a healthy lifestyle. People who exercise, eat a balanced diet without too much fatty food, do not smoke and avoid drinking too much alcohol are much less likely to have heart attacks. Regular exercise also increases the general health of the heart by making its muscle walls stronger and more efficient.

# Blood contains
# different types of cells

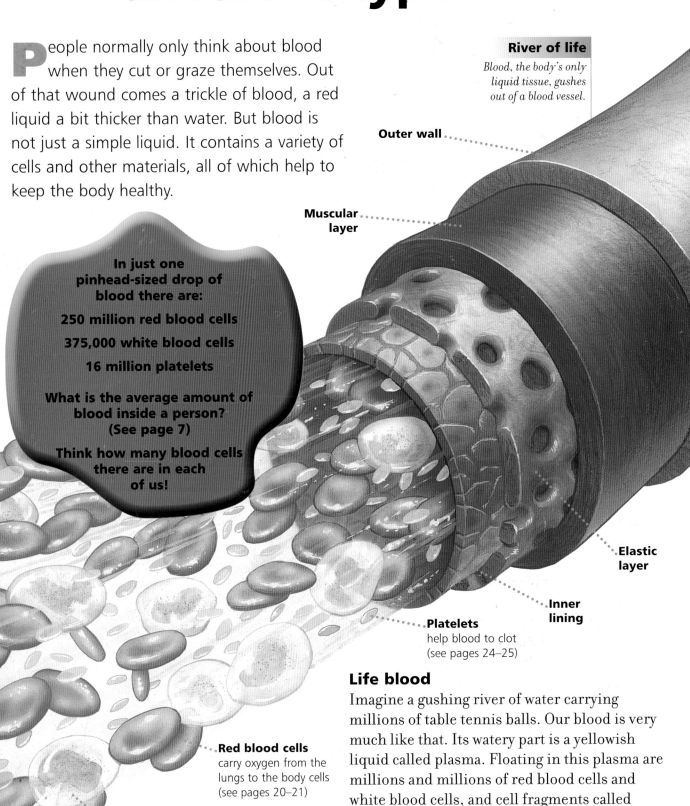

People normally only think about blood when they cut or graze themselves. Out of that wound comes a trickle of blood, a red liquid a bit thicker than water. But blood is not just a simple liquid. It contains a variety of cells and other materials, all of which help to keep the body healthy.

**River of life**

*Blood, the body's only liquid tissue, gushes out of a blood vessel.*

**Outer wall**

**Muscular layer**

**In just one pinhead-sized drop of blood there are:**

**250 million red blood cells**

**375,000 white blood cells**

**16 million platelets**

**What is the average amount of blood inside a person? (See page 7)**

**Think how many blood cells there are in each of us!**

**Elastic layer**

**Inner lining**

**Platelets**
help blood to clot
(see pages 24–25)

**Red blood cells**
carry oxygen from the lungs to the body cells
(see pages 20–21)

**White blood cells**
help defend the body against disease (see pages 22–23)

## Life blood
Imagine a gushing river of water carrying millions of table tennis balls. Our blood is very much like that. Its watery part is a yellowish liquid called plasma. Floating in this plasma are millions and millions of red blood cells and white blood cells, and cell fragments called platelets. Together with the plasma they enable blood to perform its different tasks.

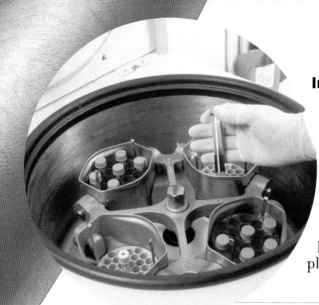

## In a spin

One way of separating the different components in blood is to use a centrifuge. This is a machine that spins the blood at high speed. When the blood has been separated, we can see that red blood cells make up about 44 per cent of blood, white blood cells and platelets make up 1 per cent, and plasma makes up 55 per cent.

## Red transporter

One of the blood's major jobs is transporting materials to and from body cells. The main function of red blood cells is to deliver oxygen to the cells. Watery plasma (about 90 per cent water) carries glucose, amino acids and other nutrients (foods) to the cells and removes wastes, such as carbon dioxide. White blood cells protect the body (see pages 22–23) and platelets help to stop wounds bleeding (see pages 24–25).

**Clearly separated**

*After they have been spun in a centrifuge, red blood cells go to the bottom, plasma stays at the top and white blood cells and platelets lie in the middle.*

## BLOOD GROUPS

Each of us belongs to one of four blood groups – A, B, AB or O. The difference between each group is caused by different 'markers' on the outside of red blood cells, which identify them as either A, B, AB or O. Doctors must always check a person's blood group if they need a blood transfusion (replacement blood is given by a donor). If a person does not receive blood from the same group, their blood can thicken, blocking blood vessels and making them very ill.

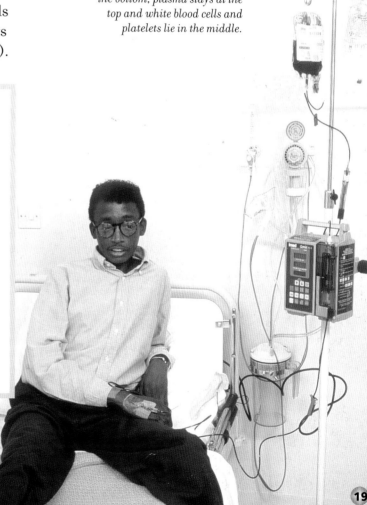

**Receiving a blood transfusion**

*During a blood transfusion a tube, attached to a bag of blood, is inserted into a vein in the arm of the patient. The replacement blood runs into their body.*

# Red blood cells
# carry oxygen

**H**ave you ever wondered why blood is red? It is because blood contains so many red blood cells, which are orangey-red in colour. Red blood cells pick up oxygen from the air we breathe into our lungs. They then rush along blood vessels at high speed to deliver that oxygen to cells throughout the body.

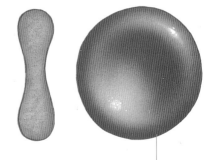

### Dimple shape

*This outside view, and section through, a red blood cell show that it has a dimpled disc shape.*

### Impressive facts

Red blood cells make up 99 per cent of cells in the blood. There are about 25 trillion (25,000,000,000,000) of them inside each person. The body produces red blood cells at the rate of 2 million every second. Each one has a lifespan of about 120 days and makes the round trip from lungs to tissues once a minute.

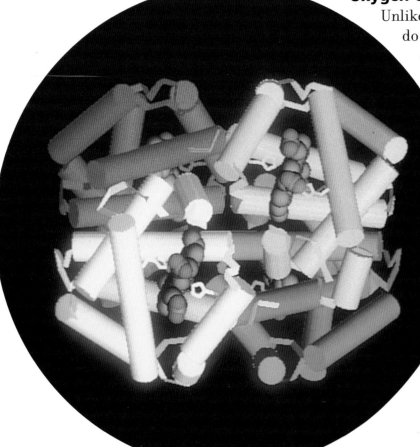

### Oxygen carriers

Unlike other body cells, red blood cells do not have a nucleus (control centre). Instead, they are packed with about 250 million molecules of a substance called haemoglobin. This gives red blood cells their colour, and carries oxygen. Haemoglobin picks up oxygen where it is plentiful – in the lungs – and releases it where it is scarce – next to the body's cells.

### Haemoglobin

*A computer graphic of a haemoglobin molecule, which is far too small to be seen by even the most powerful microscope.*

## Lining up

Capillaries, which carry red blood cells close by the body's cells, are only just wider than red blood cells. These cells squeeze and bend their way along the capillary in single file. This gives plenty of time for oxygen to pass through the wall of the capillary and into the surrounding body cells. Body cells need oxygen to release vital energy.

### Single file
*This micrograph (photograph taken using a microscope) shows red blood cells lining up in a blood capillary.*

## Shades of red

Blood becomes more or less red depending on how much oxygen it contains. Oxygen-rich blood, carried by arteries, is bright red, while oxygen-poor blood, carried by veins, is dark red. Although veins are usually coloured blue in diagrams, blood in veins is not really blue. However, dark red blood can give thin-walled veins near the skin's surface a blue appearance.

### Unusual cells
*This micrograph shows both normal and sickle-shaped red blood cells.*

## SICKLE CELLS

Some people's red blood cells are affected by sickle-cell anaemia. Some of their red blood cells form a curved, 'sickle' shape as they pass through parts of the body where oxygen levels are low. The sickle-shaped cells move less easily and can block blood vessels. This in turn blocks the blood supply and causes pain. Sickle-cell anaemia is an inherited illness, passed on from some parents to their children.

# White blood cells
## protect the body

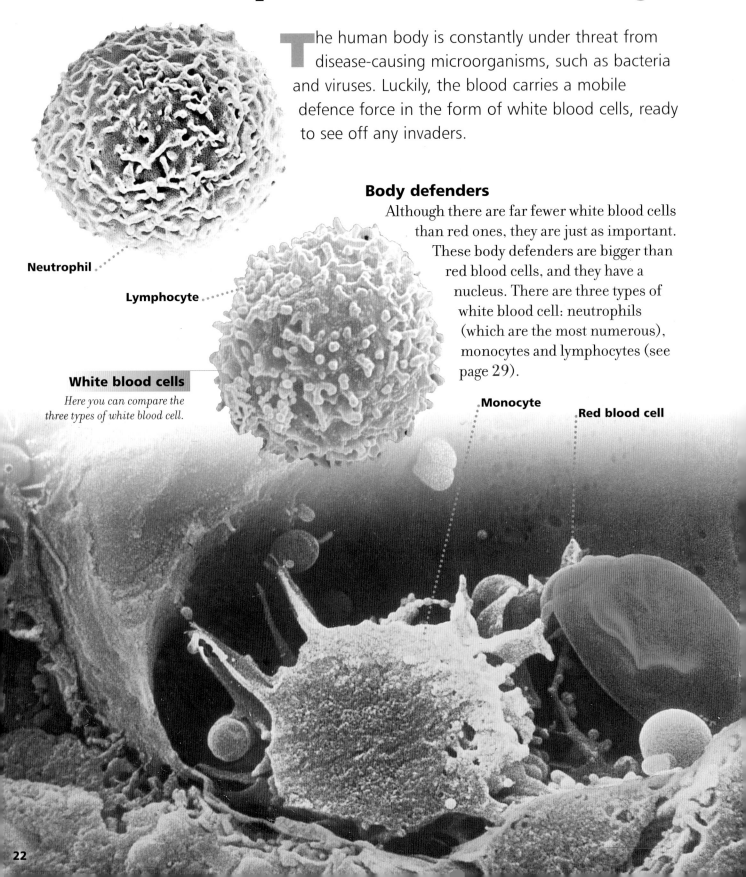

The human body is constantly under threat from disease-causing microorganisms, such as bacteria and viruses. Luckily, the blood carries a mobile defence force in the form of white blood cells, ready to see off any invaders.

**Neutrophil**

**Lymphocyte**

### White blood cells
*Here you can compare the three types of white blood cell.*

### Body defenders

Although there are far fewer white blood cells than red ones, they are just as important. These body defenders are bigger than red blood cells, and they have a nucleus. There are three types of white blood cell: neutrophils (which are the most numerous), monocytes and lymphocytes (see page 29).

**Monocyte**

**Red blood cell**

## Eating invaders

Neutrophils and monocytes are both phagocytes, or 'cell eaters'. These white blood cells specialise in finding invading microorganisms, such as bacteria, which they then surround and destroy. Neutrophils travel in the blood to a site of possible infection, such as a cut, and digest and destroy any intruding bacteria. Monocytes enter and wander through infected tissues, which they turn into macrophages ('big eaters') that engulf, digest and destroy any bacteria they find.

### Big eaters

*This hungry macrophage (large round cell) is engulfing and destroying invading germs (small green cells).*

## MAKING BLOOD CELLS

White blood cells, red blood cells and platelets are all made in the same place – red bone marrow. In young children this red, jelly-like material is found in every bone in their body. However, teenagers and adults only have red bone marrow inside certain bones, such as the skull, collarbones, shoulder blades, breastbone, backbone, pelvis and ribs. Cells inside bone marrow divide repeatedly to produce millions of blood cells every minute.

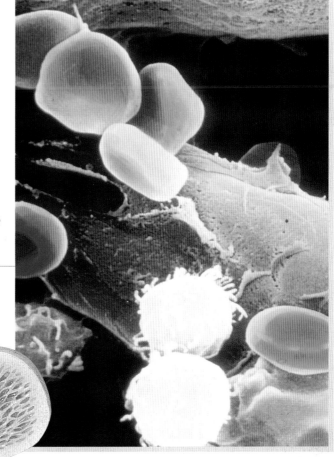

### Bone marrow

*This micrograph shows red and white blood cells being produced by red bone marrow.*

Red bone marrow

Spongy bone

# Platelets stop wounds **bleeding**

I f a water pipe gets a hole in it, water pours out. But if a blood vessel is damaged and blood flows out, the 'leak' is soon stopped. This is because blood carries its own self-repair system. This system prevents the body from losing lots of blood, which could be very dangerous.

## Vital fragments

Platelets are the key part of the blood's self-repair system. Unlike red and white blood cells, platelets are cell fragments, not complete cells. They are shaped a bit like potato crisps. If a blood vessel gets a hole in it, platelets gather at the damaged site. Here they stick to each other, forming a temporary plug that stops the bleeding.

### Sticking together

*This micrograph shows how a platelet forms projections (spikes), which allow it to stick to other platelets at a wound site.*

## Forming a clot

Once the platelet plug is formed, the next stage of wound healing happens. Sticky platelets and blood plasma release substances that turn fibrinogen, a blood-clotting protein, into hair-like threads called fibrin. Just as a fishing net traps fish, so fibrin traps blood cells to thicken the blood and make a clot, which is more permanent than the platelet plug.

### Fibrin net

*This micrograph shows red blood cells trapped in a fibrin 'net'.*

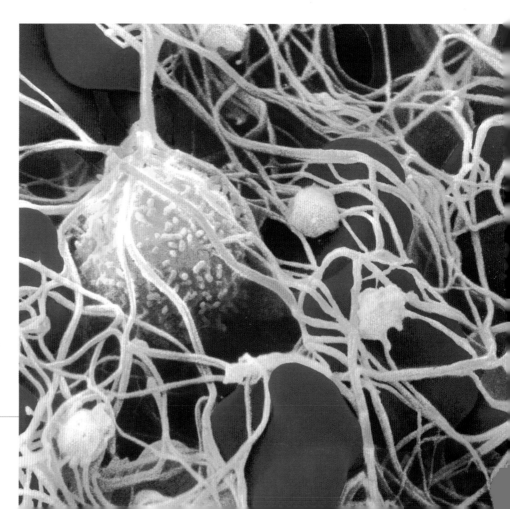

## Healing wounds

These diagrams show how a wound heals as the blood clot turns into a protective scab.

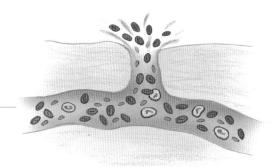

### 1. The wound bleeds

*The skin is cut and a blood vessel punctured. Platelets begin to collect at the wound site and eventually stick together to form a temporary plug.*

### 2. The blood clots

*Chemicals in the blood and from the sticky platelets convert fibrinogen into threads of fibrin. These trap blood cells to form a thick clot. White blood cells move in to attack any invading bacteria.*

### 3. A scab is formed

*The clot dries to form a hard scab. Beneath the scab, the tissue repairs itself. When healing is complete, the scab falls off.*

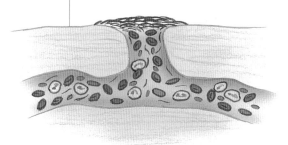

## BLOODSUCKERS

How would you feel about having a large black worm sucking your blood? Until the late 19th century, doctors used leeches (a relative of earthworms) to remove blood from their patients in the belief that it would make them better. All of the 'benefits' of using leeches were later found to be false. More recently, doctors have found another use for leeches. When they bite into the skin, leeches release a chemical that stops the blood from clotting. They can be used to remove excess blood that builds up in sensitive areas of the skin.

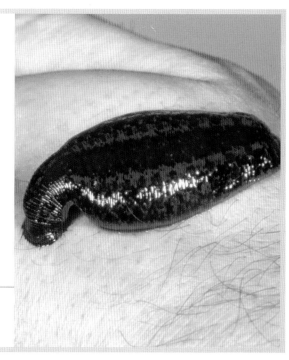

**Medicinal leech**

*This leech has bitten through human skin to feed on blood.*

# The lymphatic system supports
## the blood system

**B**lood vessels are not the only transport system in the body. A second set of tubes, called the lymphatic system, reaches all parts of the body. This system drains the body's tissues of excess liquid, and plays a vital role in protecting the body against infection.

### Making lymph
*Lymph capillaries fan out through the body's tissues to pick up excess liquid, or lymph.*

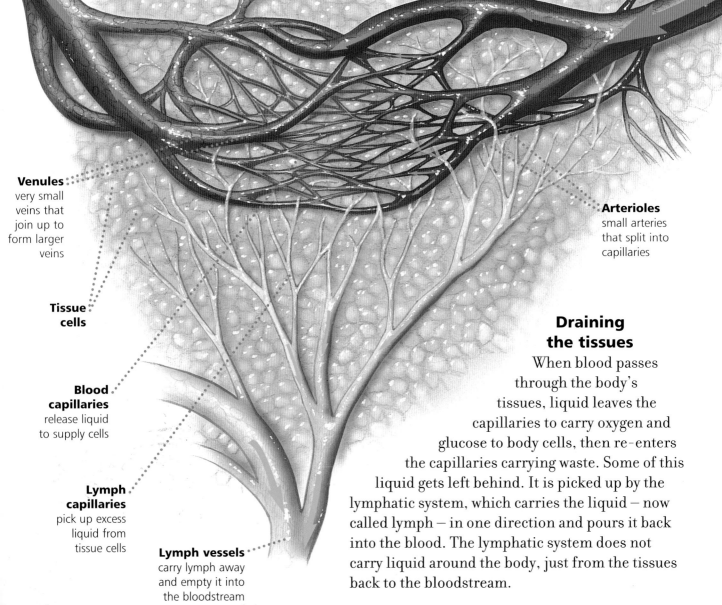

**Venules**
very small veins that join up to form larger veins

**Tissue cells**

**Blood capillaries**
release liquid to supply cells

**Lymph capillaries**
pick up excess liquid from tissue cells

**Lymph vessels**
carry lymph away and empty it into the bloodstream

**Arterioles**
small arteries that split into capillaries

### Draining the tissues
When blood passes through the body's tissues, liquid leaves the capillaries to carry oxygen and glucose to body cells, then re-enters the capillaries carrying waste. Some of this liquid gets left behind. It is picked up by the lymphatic system, which carries the liquid – now called lymph – in one direction and pours it back into the blood. The lymphatic system does not carry liquid around the body, just from the tissues back to the bloodstream.

## Vessels and capillaries

The tubes (called lymph vessels) that make up the lymphatic system branch all over the body. The smallest tubes are called lymph capillaries. Lymph capillaries merge to form larger lymph vessels, which in turn form the two largest ducts. These vessels empty the lymph into the bloodstream.

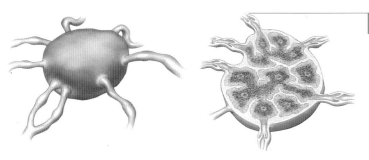

## Lymph nodes

Along the lymph vessels are bean-shaped swellings called lymph nodes, which filter the lymph as it passes through. Each lymph node contains masses of lymphocytes and macrophages (white blood cells). They target and destroy any bacteria, viruses or other microorganisms travelling in the lymph, and so help defend the body against infection. If infection does happen, it can make lymph nodes swell up — a condition better known as 'swollen glands'.

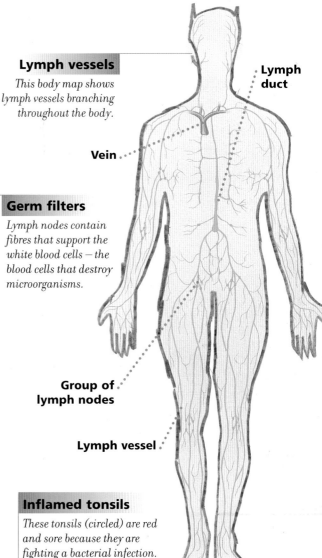

**Lymph vessels**
*This body map shows lymph vessels branching throughout the body.*

**Lymph duct**

**Vein**

**Germ filters**
*Lymph nodes contain fibres that support the white blood cells — the blood cells that destroy microorganisms.*

**Group of lymph nodes**

**Lymph vessel**

**Inflamed tonsils**
*These tonsils (circled) are red and sore because they are fighting a bacterial infection.*

## GERM CATCHERS

Tonsils, found at the back of the throat, are linked to the lymphatic system. They fight infection by trapping bacteria, which may enter the body in food or breathed-in air. Like lymph nodes, tonsils contain lots of white blood cells that destroy the bacteria. The spleen is another organ linked to the lymphatic system. The size of a fist, the spleen lies to the left of the stomach and helps to remove microorganisms from the blood.

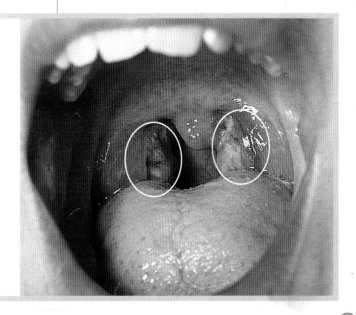

# The blood and lymphatic systems
## protect against infection

The circulatory and the lymphatic systems both play a crucial role in defending the body against microorganisms, such as bacteria and viruses. This is lucky for us, as microorganisms can be everywhere – in the air we breathe, the food we eat, the people we touch and the water we drink.

### Bacterium

*Bacteria, like this one, are the smallest living microorganisms. They are often called germs.*

**Flagella**
move the
bacterium
around

### Germ killers

*Tears not only keep the surface of the eyes clean, they also kill bacteria.*

### Outer defences

It is not that easy for microorganisms to get inside the body. The skin provides a fairly tough barrier, as do the slippery membranes that line the inside of the nose and mouth. Tears, saliva and sweat all contain germ-killing chemicals. And if invaders do slip through, germ-eating neutrophils and monocytes (see page 22) are waiting to confront them.

## Immune system

The most powerful part of the body's defences is the immune system. It consists of billions of white blood cells called lymphocytes, which are found in the circulatory and lymphatic systems, and elsewhere in the body. The immune system identifies intruding microorganisms (1), then either destroys them directly or releases antibodies (2). The immune system can also 'remember' an intruder and, if it returns, can unleash an attack with lightning speed.

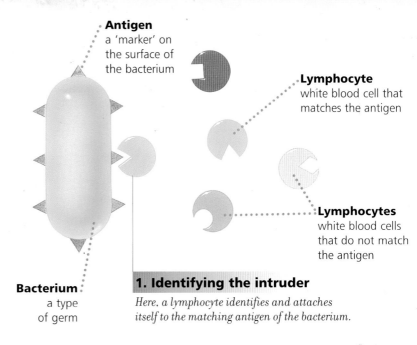

**Antigen**
a 'marker' on the surface of the bacterium

**Lymphocyte**
white blood cell that matches the antigen

**Lymphocytes**
white blood cells that do not match the antigen

**Bacterium**
a type of germ

### 1. Identifying the intruder
*Here, a lymphocyte identifies and attaches itself to the matching antigen of the bacterium.*

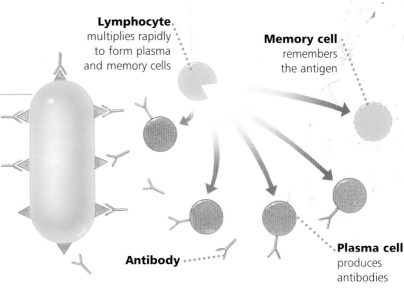

**Lymphocyte**
multiplies rapidly to form plasma and memory cells

**Memory cell**
remembers the antigen

### 2. Locking on
*Here, antibodies produced by the plasma cells lock on to the antigen of the bacterium, marking it for destruction by the germ-eating cells (see page 23).*

### Receiving an injection
*Immunisation gives the immune system a helping hand.*

**Antibody**

**Plasma cell**
produces antibodies

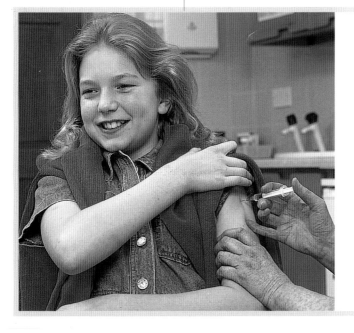

## IMMUNISATION
Children may be immunised against certain dangerous diseases, such as measles and mumps, to give extra protection. A harmless version of the germ causing a specific disease is injected into the child. This causes his or her immune system to make antibodies against the disease, but does not make them ill. But if the child is exposed to the real germ, their immune system responds immediately to destroy the infection.

# Glossary

**Amino acid** A group of organic molecules that make up proteins.

**Angiogram** A special type of X-ray that shows up blood vessels.

**Antibody** A substance released by lymphocytes that marks bacteria for destruction.

**Bacteria (singular: bacterium)** A group of living things that consist of a single, simple cell. Some bacteria cause diseases.

**Blood transfusion** The transfer of blood from one person to another.

**Blood vessel** A tube, such as an artery, vein or capillary, which carries blood through the body.

**Bone marrow** The jelly-like material inside bones. Yellow bone marrow stores fat; red bone marrow makes blood cells.

**Carbon dioxide** A gas that is the waste product of cell respiration.

**Cell** One of the tiny living units that make up all life.

**Cell respiration** The release of energy from glucose. This process occurs inside cells.

**Centrifuge** A machine that separates solids from liquids by spinning them round at high speed.

**Circulatory system** The body system that carries oxygen and other substances in the blood to all body cells, and removes waste material from the cells.

**Donor** Someone who donates their blood or organs for the treatment of others.

**Electrocardiograph** A machine that detects electrical signals produced by the heart when it beats and records them as a trace called an ECG (electrocardiogram).

**Energy** The capacity to do work.

**Fibrinogen** A blood-clotting protein that exists in the blood.

**Germs** A general term for microscopic living things (microorganisms) that cause diseases, such as bacteria and viruses.

**Glucose** The sugar obtained from food that is the body's main source of energy.

**Haemoglobin** The red substance found inside red blood cells that carries oxygen.

**Heart rate** The number of times the heart beats over a period of time (usually per minute).

**Immunisation** The process by which a person is protected against certain germs and diseases.

**Micrograph** A photograph taken using a microscope.

**Microorganism** A tiny living thing, such as a bacterium, only visible under the microscope.

**Molecule** A simple chemical structure.

**Muscle** Body tissue that can use energy to contract (get shorter) and move the body.

**Nerve impulse** A tiny electrical signal.

**Nucleus** Part of a cell that controls the cell's activities.

**Oxygen** A gas found in the air that is essential for releasing the energy needed for life. This energy release occurs during aerobic cell respiration.

**Pulse** The beat produced as blood surges along an artery after a heartbeat.

**Sensor** Part of the body that detects changes inside or outside the body.

**Skeletal muscle** Muscle attached to bone that allows the body to move.

**Sphygmomanometer** An instrument that measures blood pressure.

**Stethoscope** Instrument used to listen to the heart or to breathing noises.

**System** A collection of body organs that work together to carry out a particular job.

**Tissue** A collection of the same, or similar, cells that work together to perform a specific task.

**Transplant** The transfer of an organ, such as the heart, from one person to another.

**Trillion** A very large number. One trillion (1,000,000,000,000) is the same as one million million.

**Virus(es)** A group of living particles that cause disease in humans and other living things.

**X-ray** A type of radiation used to look at body parts.

# Find out more

These are just some of the websites where you can find out more information about the heart. Many of the websites also provide information and illustrations about other systems and processes of the human body.

**Note to parents and teachers**
Every effort has been made by the Publishers to ensure that these websites are suitable for children; that they are of the highest educational value, and that they contain no inappropriate or offensive material. However, because of the nature of the Internet, it is impossible to guarantee that the contents of these sites will not be altered. We strongly advise that Internet access is supervised by a responsible adult.

**www.medtropolis.com**
This Virtual Body website includes an animation of the heart in action that can be speeded up or slowed down, as would happen during or after exercise.

**www.hyperstaffs.info/ science/work/durber**
Use this website to see an animation of how the blood transports oxygen, carbon dioxide and glucose, and interact to keep 'Ernie' alive.

**www.smm.org/heart**
Interact with this Habits of the Heart website to, for example, find the heartbeat with a virtual stethoscope.

**www.brainpop.com/ health/circulatory/**
Movies, quizzes and lots more information about the circulatory system, blood pressure, blood donations, and more.

**www.bbc.co.uk/ education/medicine/**
This 'Medicine Through Time' website includes Dr William Harvey's discovery of blood circulation and much more about anatomy and surgery during the 17th century.

**http://vilenski.org/ science/humanbody**
Join in the Human Body Adventure to discover more about the blood, heart and how other parts of the body work.

**www.planet-science.com/ outthere/index.html?page =/outthere/bodybeat/ fitness_factory/heart.html**
This website investigates the heart, fitness and exercise.

**http://fi.edu/biosci/blood/**
This Franklin Institute website provides highly detailed information about the heart and circulatory system.

**www.amnh.org/ nationalcenter/infection**
An interactive website all about microbes, including those germs that can invade the body and cause diseases if not stopped by the body's defence systems.

**www.childrenfirst.nhs.uk/ kids/health/illnesses/ transfusions.html**
This website provides lots of information about blood transfusions, sickle-cell anaemia, and other conditions affecting the circulatory system.

**http://kidshealth.org/ teen/your_body/ body_basics/spleen.html**
How the spleen and lymphatic system works are just some of the body parts explained here, along with links to the circulatory system.

# Index